By Jan Glaesel

The Complete Method For Trumpet

IMPROVE YOUR GAME

PEDAL-TONE STUDIES & 10 DAILY ROUTINES

Volume II

WRITTEN BY: JAN GLAESEL
COPYRIGHT © 2012:
JAN GLAESEL / JGMUSIK APS DK
WWW.TRUMPETGAME.COM

INDEX - VOLUME II

COLOPHONE: TITEL: IMPROVE YOUR GAME - VOLUME II - 1. EDITION · AUTHOR: JAN GLAESEL · PUBLISHER & COPYRIGHT: JGMUSIK APS · DK 2012 · ISBN: ISBN 978-87 92945-01-3 · LAYOUT: AJOUR GRAFISK DESIGN · COVERPHOTO: HANS OLE MADSEN · WEBSITE: WWW.TRUMPETGAME.COM · CONTACT: INFO@TRUMPETGAME.COM

FOREWORD:

This is actually the second time I'm writing this foreword. Right now I'm sitting at Starbucks in Central Pattaya, Thailand. I've just spent the last two weeks here in solitude in this wonderful country, away from home, work, phones and daily decisions, to finally finish my Trumpet Method Book "Improve Your Game – The Complete Method Book for Trumpet"

This project started in 2004, and the first time I wrote this foreword was in 2008 somewhere in the airspace between the U.S. and Denmark. I had been working in Las Vegas as a musical director for one of my Danish friends, a musical show genius, who wanted to try things out "over there". In my spare time, I collected all my notes on practising into one huge pile, and then thought, "That's it – the book is done". But boy was I wrong. When I got back home, I started looking at my "new book" – and it was a complete mess. It took me another four years to complete this project, inventing new systems and exercises to make the project come together. Now I have a complete overview of my material, have tried most of my ideas on myself, and now feel confident knowing that I have something of real value to pass on to my fellow trumpet players.

HERE IS MY STORY:

While playing drums at the age of 6 in the Tivoli Boys Guard in Copenhagen, I practised the trumpet, and 8 years old I got my spot in the marching band and just fell in love with the instrument. I spent 10 years in Tivoli and by the time I retired at 16 years of age, I was a semi-professional musician. I could sight-read music, follow a conductor, learned to be on time, and learned all of the other things that make you successful in the business. But suddenly, I was "unemployed".

In high school I joined some different bands playing all different kinds of music. In the beginning I had a huge problem: There was no music to read!!! My whole life I had played from written music, and now suddenly I had to just play something and improvise. I was completely lost for a while, but with time came the courage to jump without a parachute. It sounded awful, and other trumpet players would probably have been kicked out of the band (unless you had a van or a rehearsal room), but I had something else. Due to my training in The Tivoli

Boys Guard, I had the power and technique to play all the high stuff, and I could play for hours without getting tired. On top of that I knew my theory, and had a flair for composing and arranging. So, whenever somebody needed an arrangement or song – they knew who to call. I stayed in business and started getting a lot of work. In 1979 I had the fortune to be approached by the Big Band Guru Thad Jones, who at that time lived in Denmark wanted to form a Danish/American big band - Eclipse. For the next 3 years I learned everything about being a big band section-player. That was an experience of a lifetime.

To cut a long story short, I ended up as Musical Director on Danish National TV and was placed in charge of some of the biggest acts in the entertainment business in Denmark. I became known as the guy who could play trumpet with one hand, and conduct with the other – and actually I can. I formed my own company writing music for feature film and commercials – boy I've written a lot of those.

A day is only 24 hours – that's a fact. So with a schedule as busy as mine has been for the last 20 years, I of course had to cut some corners. Since practising didn't pay bills, and wasn't fun – I cut down on that. For many years I never practised. I just played, played and played, because I didn't have the time to invest.

THIS WAS THE WAY IT USED TO BE

After months of preparation, writing, rehearsing and just minutes before the first downbeat on the opening night of a show, I would ask the band: "Has anybody seen my horn?" I would find it, oil the valves and just give it a kick in the #¤%&, and would (barely) survive that first night. After a couple of shows it would get easier, and no one would suspect that I never practiced. The truth of the matter was that if you had given me a simple Danish Folksong and asked me to play it mezzopiano – I would have tanked completely.

THE CROSSROAD

By 2004, we had played thousands of shows during a 15 year period so we decided to take an indefinite break. This wasn't a big problem for me as I had all my writing, arranging and producing jobs. BUT – what about my beloved trumpet? Now I had two options:

SELL MY HORNS – OR – START TO PRACTICE!!

This book is the proof of my decision. The way back to falling in love with my instrument again has been long, frustrating, and hard, but above all – really, really rewarding.

THE FIRST DAY AT "WORK"

After making the decision to find out how good a trumpet player I could have been, I started to practice. I had promised myself to practice at least one hour a day, and that sounded within reach for me. Then I experienced the scariest moment in my professional life. I went to my studio, got out the trumpet and stared at it for a loooong time, not knowing what to play. I played some scales – enough to make an hour pass by. But when I looked at the clock, only 3 minutes had passed. I put down the horn, and gave up.

I've never been good at defeat, so the next day I found my very old copy of Arban's Complete Conservatory Method For Trumpet. The Arban had been the bible for me in the Tivoli Boys Guard. I knew my way around it, but it had been a long time since I looked at it. I put together a one hour program of exercises from the Arban book, and had a really hard time getting it together. On the negative side it soon occurred to me what a lousy technique I had, but on the positive side, I started to improve – fast. Nothing is more rewarding than when you put in the effort and start getting results.

At a lecture in Copenhagen, American Business Coach **Keith Cunningham** came with a statement that really was an eye-opener for me. He said:

"IF YOU HAVE A TALENT, NO MATTER WHAT IT IS, AND SPEND 3 HOURS A DAY FOR 3 YEARS ON IMPROVING YOUR SKILLS, YOU WILL AFTER THOSE 3 YEARS BE IN THE TOP 100 IN YOUR FIELD - WORLDWIDE!!"

An average lifespan is roughly 700,000 hours and you only have to spend 3,285 hours of those to get in the top 100 worldwide. How easy is that!! OK – if you want to stay at the top 100 or get to #1, you have to put in a lot of additional hours – but you get the picture.

Since I restarted my practice career, I've studied a lot of books from great brass players, including Allen Vizzutti, Arturo Sandoval, Schlossberg, Clark, Herring, Stamp, Caruso, Claude Gordon – you name it. I also picked a lot of brains, met and played with some terrific trumpet players to get the material together that helped point me in the right direction, and I really want to share this research and material with you.

Let me get one thing straight:
I CAN'T PLAY EVERYTHING I WROTE IN THIS BOOK!!!!

If I only wrote exercises that I could play – I wouldn't learn anything. But I'm getting there: hour by hour, day by day, exercise by exercise. The day I can play everything in this book, I will write another. Here is a promise to you. If you can play the "Lyrical Interval Etude" that I wrote and dedicated to Mr. Malcolm McNab (in Vol. 4) I'll write a new one dedicated to you. (I can't play it – yet)

At age 54 I'm all fired up about playing and practicing my horn and I'm planning on improving my game for the next many years. I can't tell you when I'll stop – and as long as the horn sounds a little bit better every day I pick it up – I'll keep blowing.

JAN GLAESEL
Copenhagen, Denmark - 2012

HOW TO USE THIS BOOK

This book has been divided into 4 separate and independent volumes so that you can dig into specific areas instead of having to buy one large book just for one section, such as "The 10 Daily Routines" or "All Scales".

- **Vol. I – Warm-ups, interval & Slurring Exercises**
- **Vol. II – Pedal-tones & Low Notes / The 10 Daily Routines**
- **Vol. III – All Scales / Transposition & Dexterity Studies**
- **Vol. IV – Tonguing / Target, Precision & Endurance /Performance / Melodies & Etudes**

IMPORTANT!!

I've come up with three basic "rules" that apply to this book. They are:

1.   REST ALMOST AS MUCH AS YOU PLAY

Practising can be harder than playing a gig. When I started this journey, I would practise one hour a day. My mistake was that I played for a full hour without resting at all. So when 60 minutes were up, I was done, and after a couple of weeks my lips were like two bricks. If you want to practice playing your horn for one hour – you should practice for two hours. Get the idea? Rest is important.

2.   3 STRIKES AND YOU'RE OUT!!

This needs explanation. When you look through the book you will probably be a little intimidated over all the high notes and tiring phrases – don't be. All exercises are written so that every trumpet player on an intermediate level can benefit from them – as long as they practice using this *"3 strikes and you're out"* rule.

Whenever you reach your current range limit – **give it three attempts, then stop.** The next day you can give it a shot again. In a few days, you will experience that what was once impossible, is now a walk in the park.

Exercises like this are divided into two or three sections. If I state, "Don't continue beyond this point if not within your range", stay within you range a couple of more days, and it will come. Remember: **"Good Things Come To Those Who Wait."** And HEY!! If the whole high note concept isn't something interesting to you, don't go there!! Simply skip those exercises, and let your normal high C be the top of your range. Remember:
"No note is so high, that it can't be played an octave or two down"!!

3. PUT AS MUCH MUSIC AS POSSIBLE INTO EVERYTHING YOU PLAY

Let's face it – 95% of these exercises are plain boring when you just look at them. But if you try to put as much music or feeling into them when playing, you can make them come to life. On top of that you should play everything with the most beautiful sound you can imagine. These two things together are essential for getting to the point where time just flies when you practice.

In the Chapter on **Performance in Vol. 4**, I will share with you hundreds of ideas that made sense to me about trumpet playing that I picked up around fellow trumpet players and the internet. I call this, "Spiritual Tapas". In this same section, a good friend and fellow trumpet player **Jon Gorrie** will give you an introduction to his book "Performing In The Zone" – a book all performers should read.

LAST RULES:
"TREAT YOURSELF TO SOME OF THE ETUDES IN THE BACK OF EACH VOLUME"
&
"TAKE A DAY OFF FROM TRUMPET PLAYING EVERY WEEK!!"
LET'S PRACTICE!!

INTRODUCTION TO SELECTED CHAPTERS VOLUME II

INTRODUCTION TO PEDAL-TONES PAGE 12

Read carefully the "Introduction To Pedal-tones" on page 12.

PEDAL-TONES STUDIES PAGE 13

Ex.1 This exercise takes you chromatically down from your low C. From low F and down focus on hitting the pitches as clean as possible. Keep the same embouchure all the way.

Ex.2 Have focus on slurring the octaves as clean as possible. Try to keep the same embouchure all the way.

Ex.3 Now we expand with an extra octave. It's ok to slow it down so you really can focus on

10 DAILY ROUTINES - WEEK BY WEEK PAGE 16 - 89

OBS!! Before starting on the Daily Routines you should go through the Pedal Tones section

Together these 10 Daily Routine is a powerful tool to improvement. By Daily Routines I don't mean that you absolutely have to play one every single day - but as all trumpet players have, there are days where you don't know what to practise - here they come in real handy. And whenever you feel a little out of shape, for instance after a vacation, build a suitable program around them. BUT - first time you get into these Daily Routine, you should create a program for a longer period of time and have the pleasure of feeling the rapid improvement by using them.

Start of course with "Daily Routine - Week 1" and play that for a week or so, until you can play it all the way through and remember the "3 strikes" rule. When you are comfortable with this - move on to "Daily Routine - Week 2" and so on.

And by the way - I hate to read low pedal-tones in there right notation, so I use a lot of 8va basso notation for your convenience.

HERE'S A RUN THROUGH OF THE CONSTRUCTION OF THE EXERCISES.

Each Daily Routine consist of two main parts:

DAILY ROUTINE - PART 01.

A daily thematic expanding routine in three parts.
Ex.1 = Phrase A. - Ex.2 = Phrase A&B - Ex.3 = Phrase A,B&C
All thematic routines with one exception (Week 6) goes round the circle of 5th for variation and constant change in register.

DAILY ROUTINE - PART 02.

A daily slurring routine in 2 or 3 parts.

DIRECTIONS FOR THE INDIVIDUAL EXERCISES.
DAILY ROUTINE - WEEK 1,2,3,4 - 8 AND 10:

This is actually the basic layout of the whole concept of all the Daily Routines. Read it through without playing ,so you get the fundamentals of the exercises. if I write "Opt.8vb........" it optional. Tempos are only suggestions. After the Daily Slur exercises, end with playing the "cool down phrase" and remember to take a good break before continuing.

THE EXCEPTIONS:
DAILY ROUTINE - WEEK 5 - PAGE 41

This exercise focuses on jumping i octaves. Ex. 1 is just jumping one octave. Ex. 2 is jumping 2 octaves - one at a time going down. Ex.3 is also jumping 2 octaves, first 1 octave up - and then 2 down finishing of with a diminished appegio going up. The high endings are optional.

DAILY ROUTINE . WEEK 6 - ENDURANCE - PAGE 48

In this exercise it's crucial that you follow my rule number 2 :"3 strikes and you're out". Otherwise you'll hurt yourself, and that's definitely not the object of this exercise. The object is to strengthen your chops and the only way to do that, is NOT to overdo it. Whenever you hit the wall - give it 3 attempt - THEN STOP!! I promise you "Good things come to the ones that wait".

DAILY ROUTINE - WEEK 7 - PAGE 53

Actually it follows the basic layout of the rest of the routines, but it has a little bonus. After The Daily Slurs, there's a Expanding Major Scale exercise. It's a simple scale over a sixth stretching from G to E, next one expands in each end, from F# to F#, then F to G and so on. Last one expands from G below the system to double G. Again remember rule nr. 2: "3 strikes and you're out".

DAILY ROUTINE - WEEK 9 - PAGE 73

Same as Week 7 with and added bonus in the slur section. The slur exercises are not in intervals, but they're chromatic and expanding. Daily Slur I is over 2 octaves, and Daily Slur II is over 3 octaves. The expansion is only in one end - every version starts at G below the staff and expands with a semitone at the top. Remember - "3 strikes and you're out".

TREAT YOURSELF WITH SOME OF THE MUSICAL ETUDES & STUDIES PG. 92 - 95

LET'S GET GOING - AND REMEMBER THESE WISE WORDS:

"YOU CAN'T HIRE SOMEONE TO PRACTISE FOR YOU "
QUOTE: H. JACKSON BROWN JR.

Introduction To Pedal-tones

Lowest actual notes on trumpet							False Pedal-tones					True fundamental pitches						
C	B	Bb	A	Ab	G	F#	F	E	Eb	D	Db	C	B	Bb	A	Ab	G	F#
0	2	1	12	23	13	123	1	12	23	13	123	0	2	1	12	23	13	123

What are pedal-tones and what purpose do they serve? If you look at the example above you can see many low notes extending below the normal range of the trumpet. Why are they called pedal-tones? They derived their name from the low notes played with the feet on an organ.

From middle C to low F# are actual tones within the trumpet's range.
But from low F to Db, I refer to them as "False Pedal-tones". Here is the explanation.

By pressing the valves, in various combinations, there are 7 different tones in the harmonic series descending from middle C to low F#.

1. valve lower the pitch with a whole tone
2. valve lower the pitch with a semi-tone
3. valve lower the pitch with a whole tone + a semi-tone

In various combinations, the valves gives you the seven different fundamental pitches in the harmonic series. When you go from your lowest actual note on the horn, low F#, to F, you go from a fundamental pitch to the first false pedal tone F. Why is it false? Well, it's because it belongs to the fundamental pitch Bb, so you have to "lip" the note down to get the right pitch. If you continue down, you have to do this all the way to pedal C where you again hit a fundamental pitch.

If you want to recieve all the benefits from playing pedal-tones it's crucial that you play all true fundamental pitches as such, and with the correct fingering. For some, it's easier to play pedal-tones with false fingerings. Played in this manner, you do not receive all the benefits of playing it correctly. So continuing down from pedal C, play as fundamental pitches and use correct fingerings.

Pedal-tones are supposed to sound awful, so don't get frustrated and don't over-do it!!

I despise reading low notes. All those ledger lines! Very frustrating! So throughout this chapter,
I will always notate as indicated in the example below:

C	B	Bb	A	Ab	G	F#	F	E	Eb	D	Db	C	B	Bb	A	Ab	G	F#
0	2	1	12	23	13	123	1	12	23	13	123	0	2	1	12	23	13	123

Pedal-tones Studies

Try to play this chromatic scale with a good sound and as evenly as possible.

Now you get the idea with the false pedals, so I'll stop marking the fingerings.

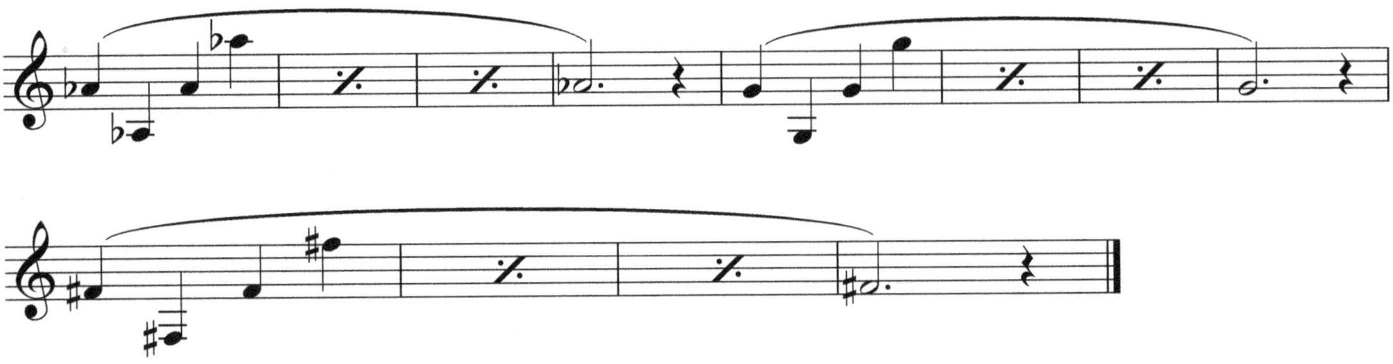

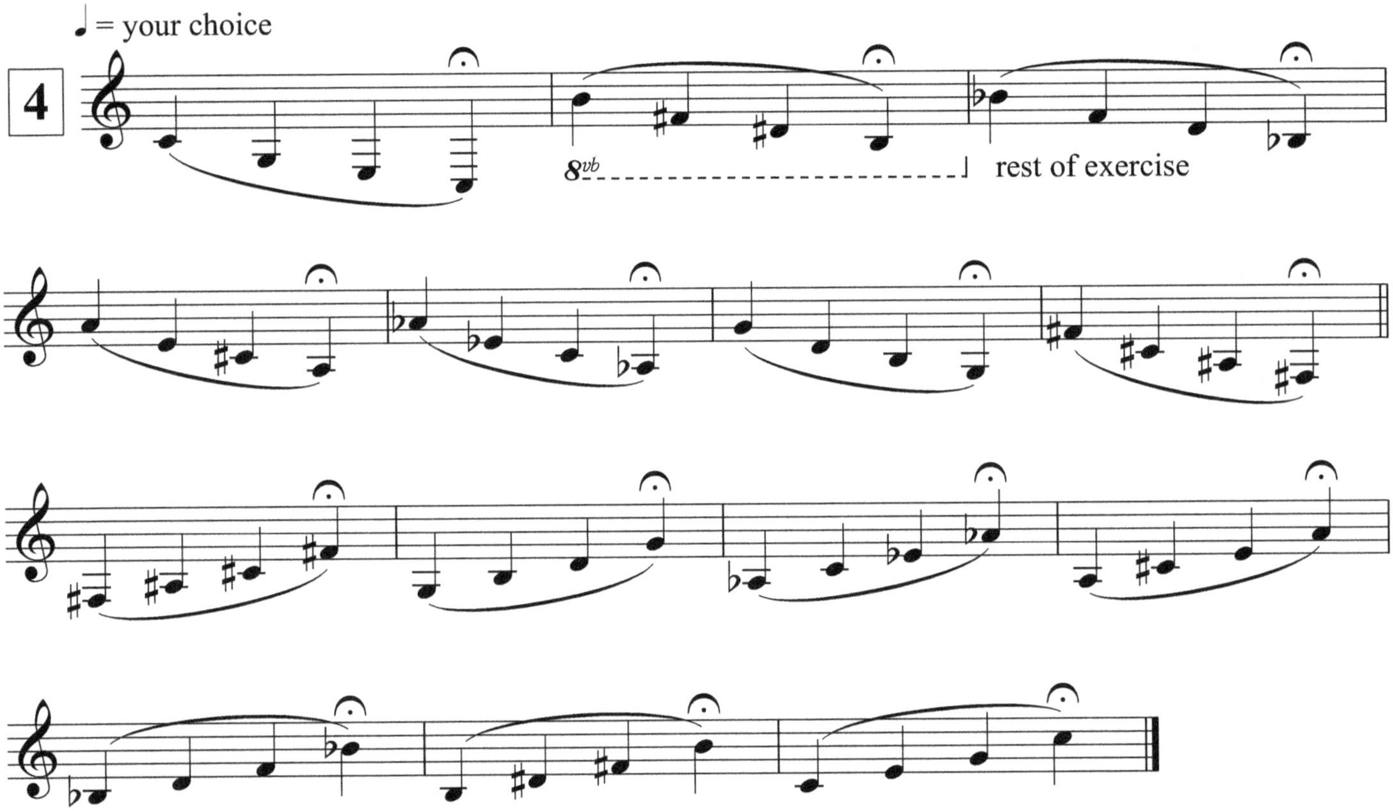

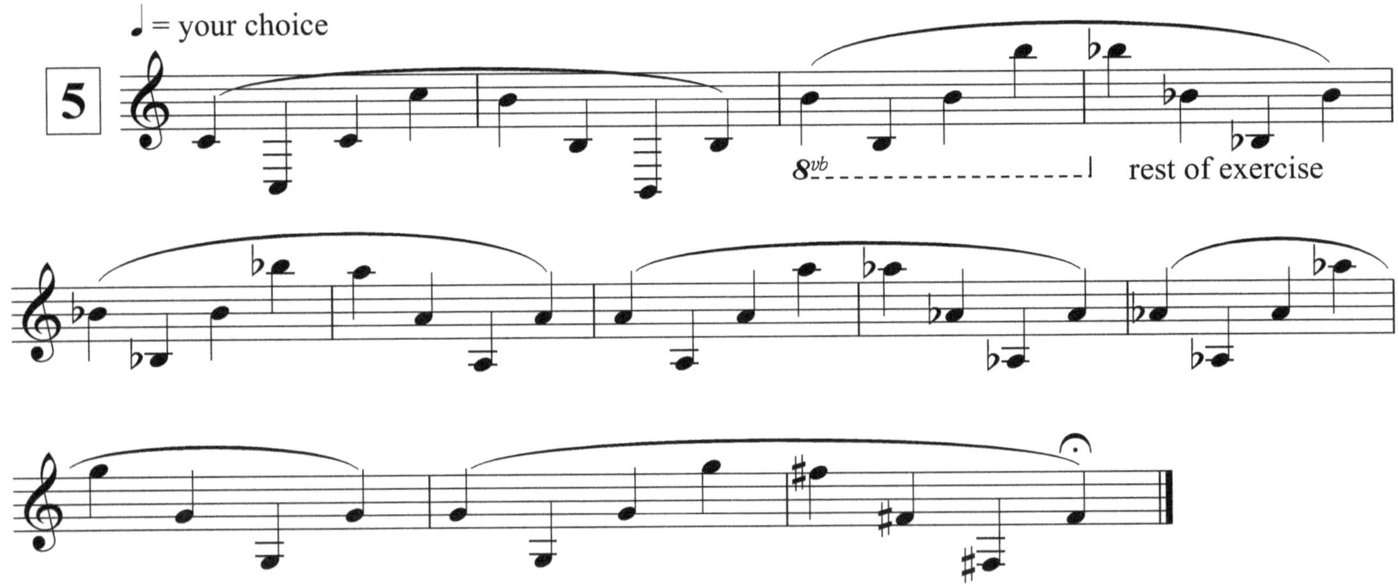

Rest Your Chops Before Continuing!

A routine a day keeps the doctor away!!

Daily Routine - Week 01

(Please read "Introduction to chapters" for reference - see index)

A♭
8vb
D♭
8vb
G♭
Opt. 8vb
B
8vb
E
8vb
A
8vb
D
8vb
G
8vb
C
8vb
F
8vb
B♭
8vb
E♭
8vb

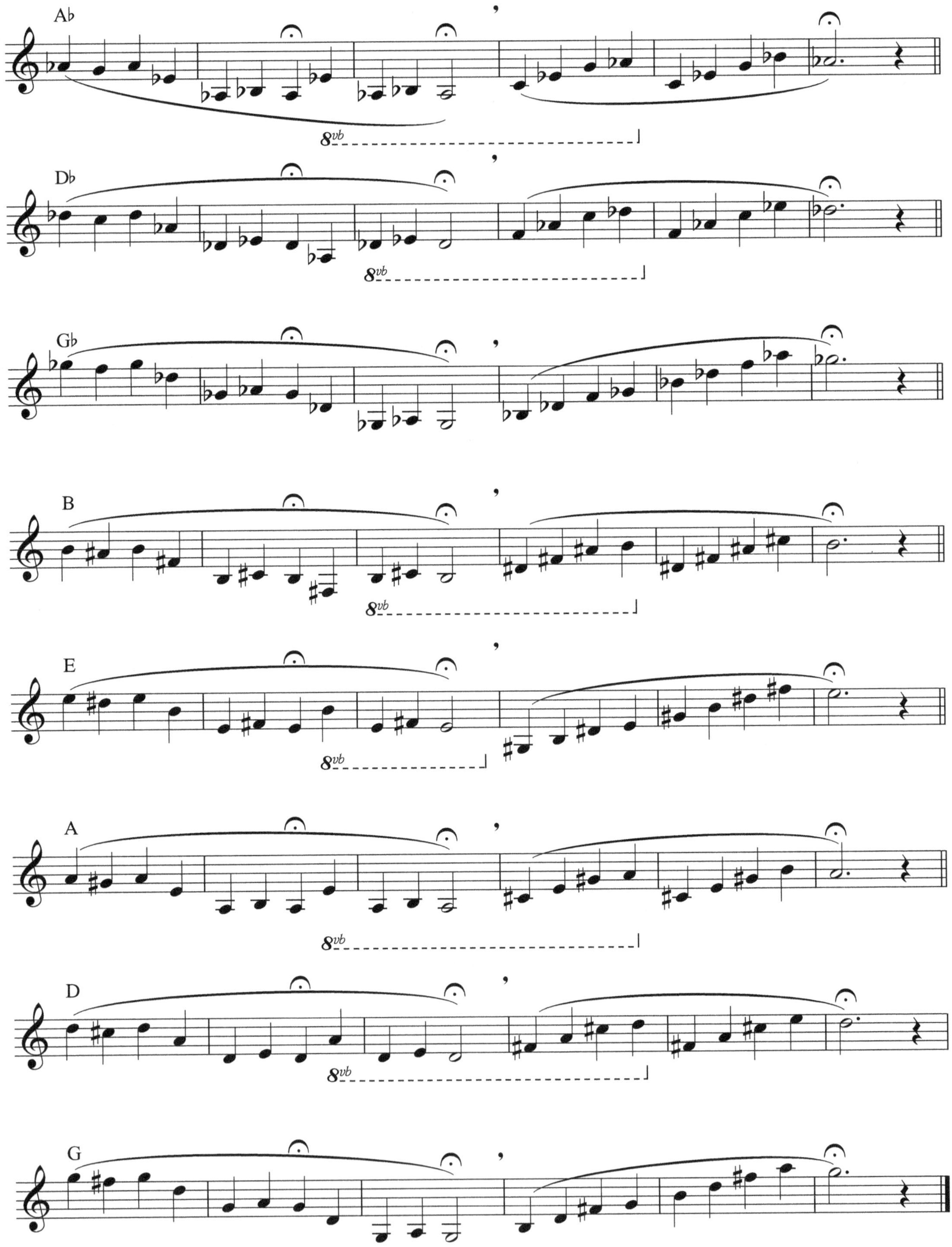
A♭
8vb
D♭
8vb
G♭
B
8vb
E
8vb
A
8vb
D
8vb
G

Daily Slurs - Week 01

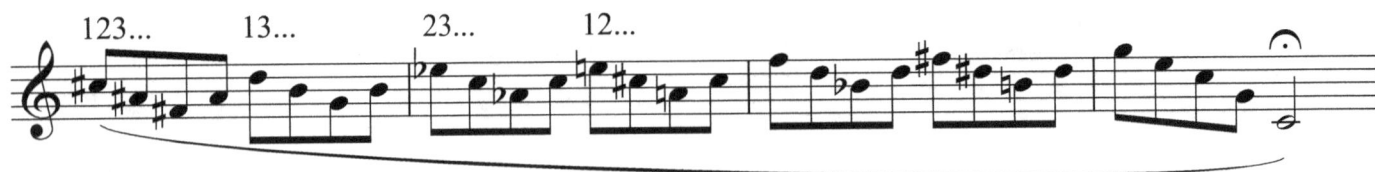

Cool down phrase

Take a 5-10 minute break before continuing.

While resting, keep the energy flowing.
Do something productive!

Daily Routine - Week 02

(Please read "Introduction to chapters" for reference - see index)

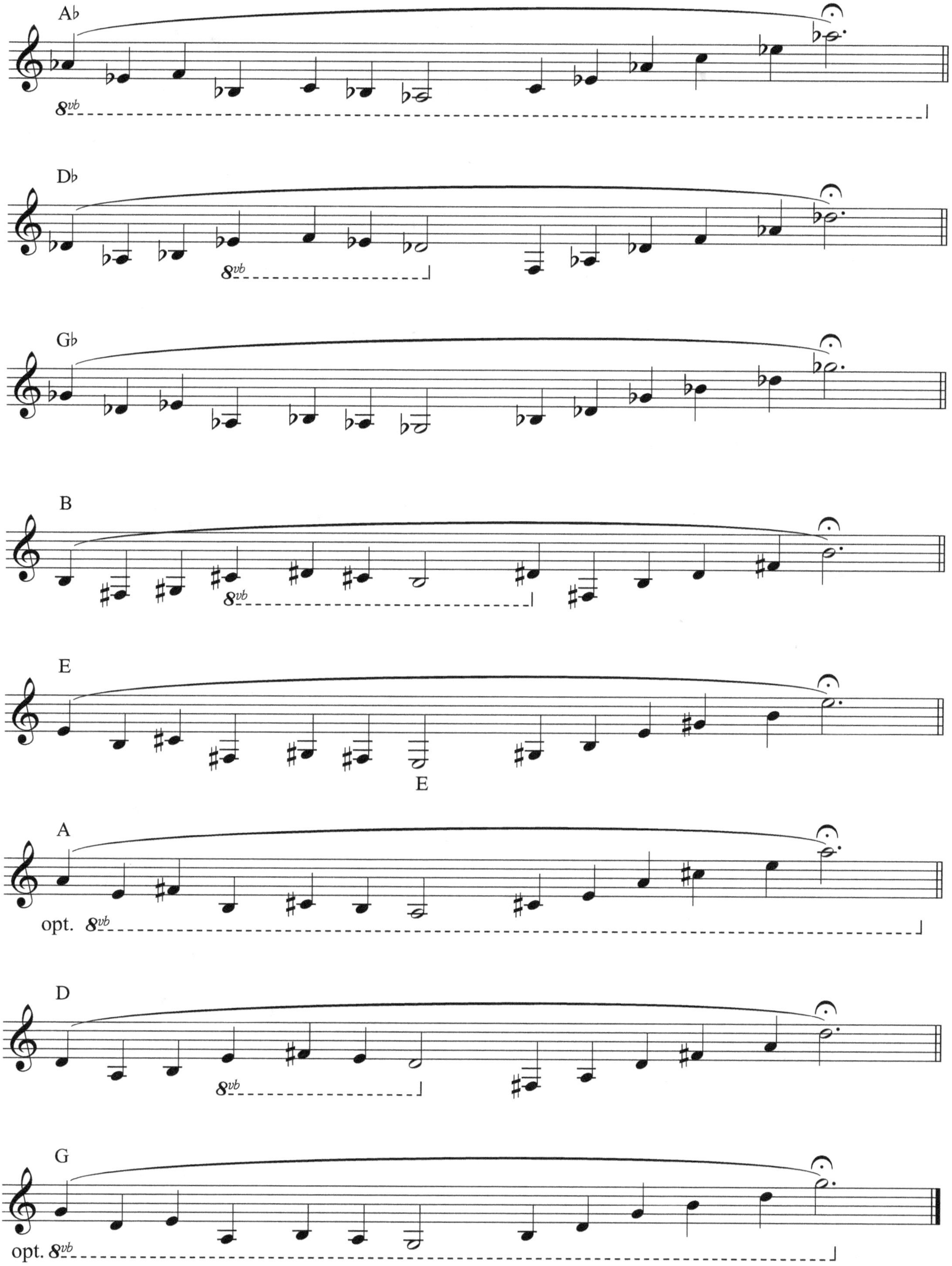
A♭
8vb
D♭
8vb
G♭
B
8vb
E
E
A
opt. 8vb
D
8vb
G
opt. 8vb

24

Rest 5-10 minutes before continuing.
Have a cup of coffee or surf the internet.

Daily Slur - Week 02

Cool down phrase

Take a 5-10 minute break. Go on facebook!!

28

By now you're probably gettin' the hang of it.

Daily Routine - Week 03

(Please read "Introduction to chapters" for reference - see index)

© 2012 Improve Your Game - JGMusik ApS DK

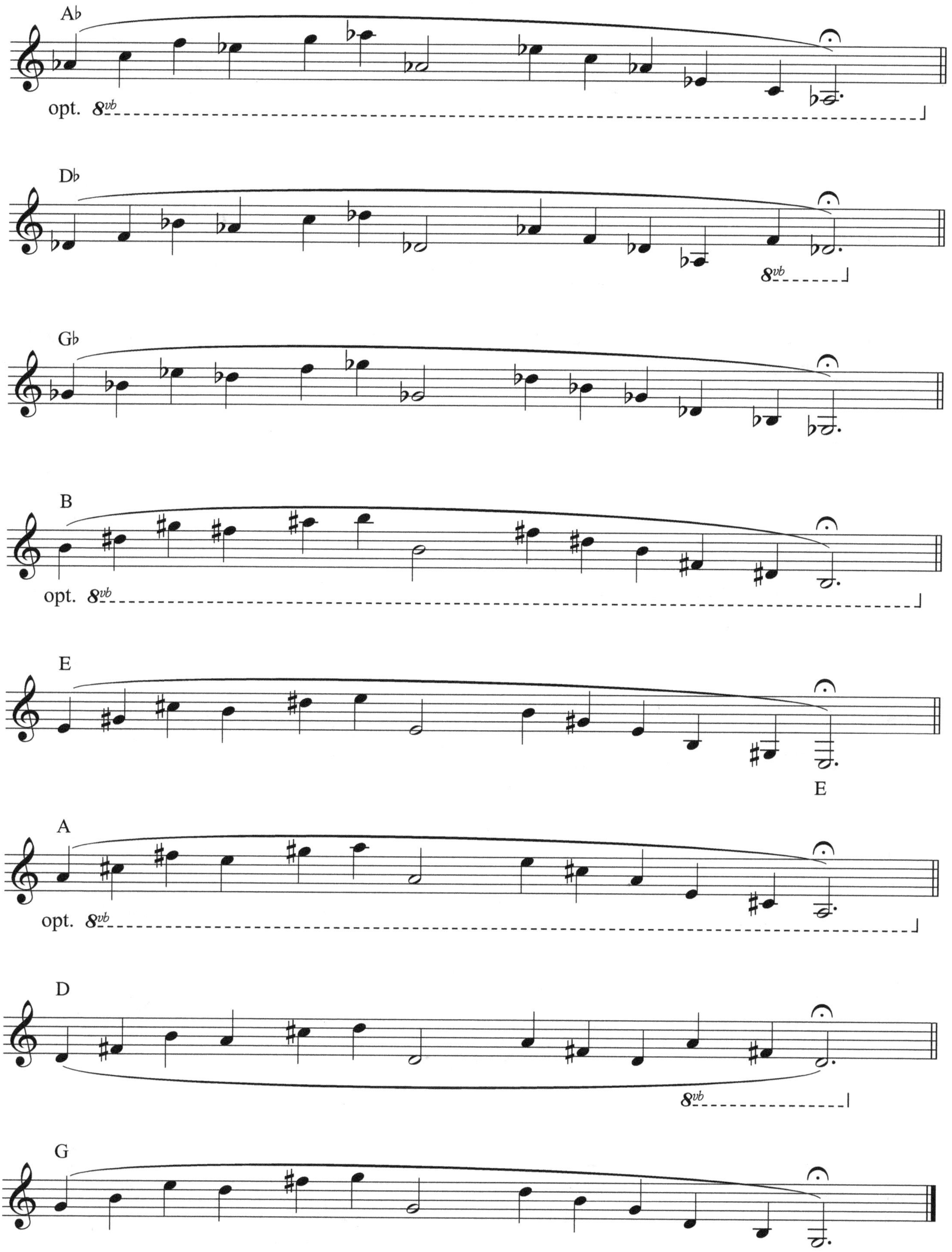
A♭
opt. 8vb
D♭
8vb
G♭
B
opt. 8vb
E
E
A
opt. 8vb
D
8vb
G

30

E

A

opt. 8vb

D

G

Cool down phrase

f

Rest 5-10 minutes before continuing.
What about a little time on twitter?

Daily Slurs - Week 03

33

Conclusion:

Conclusion:

Cool down phrase

Take a 5-10 minute break.
If you have a Myspace profile - go there.

Don't read - think!!

Daily Routine - Week 04

(Please read "Introduction to chapters" for reference - see index)

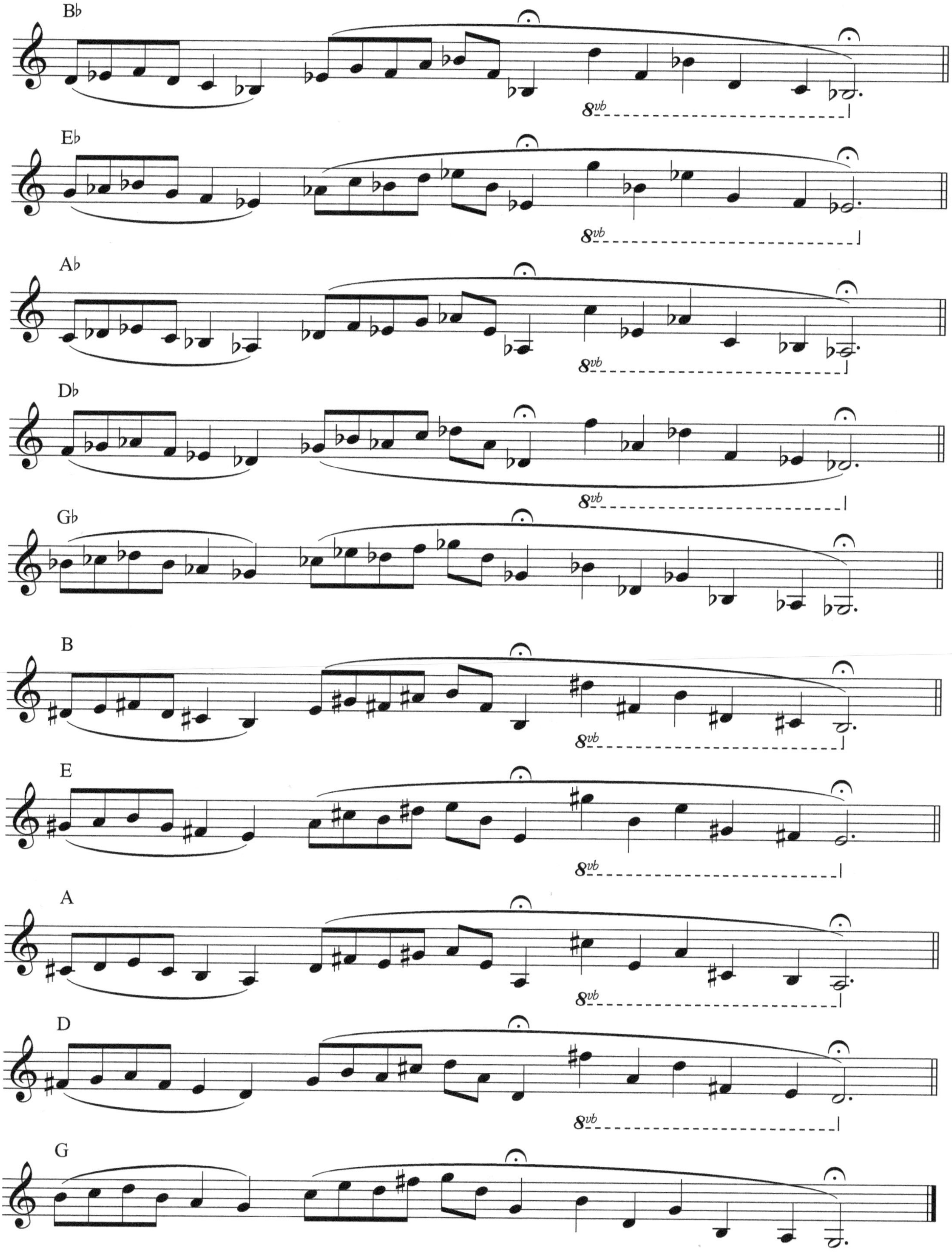
B♭
8vb
E♭
8vb
A♭
8vb
D♭
8vb
G♭
B
8vb
E
8vb
A
8vb
D
8vb
G

36

3

C

8vb

(8)

F

Bb

8vb

(8)

Eb

8vb

(8)

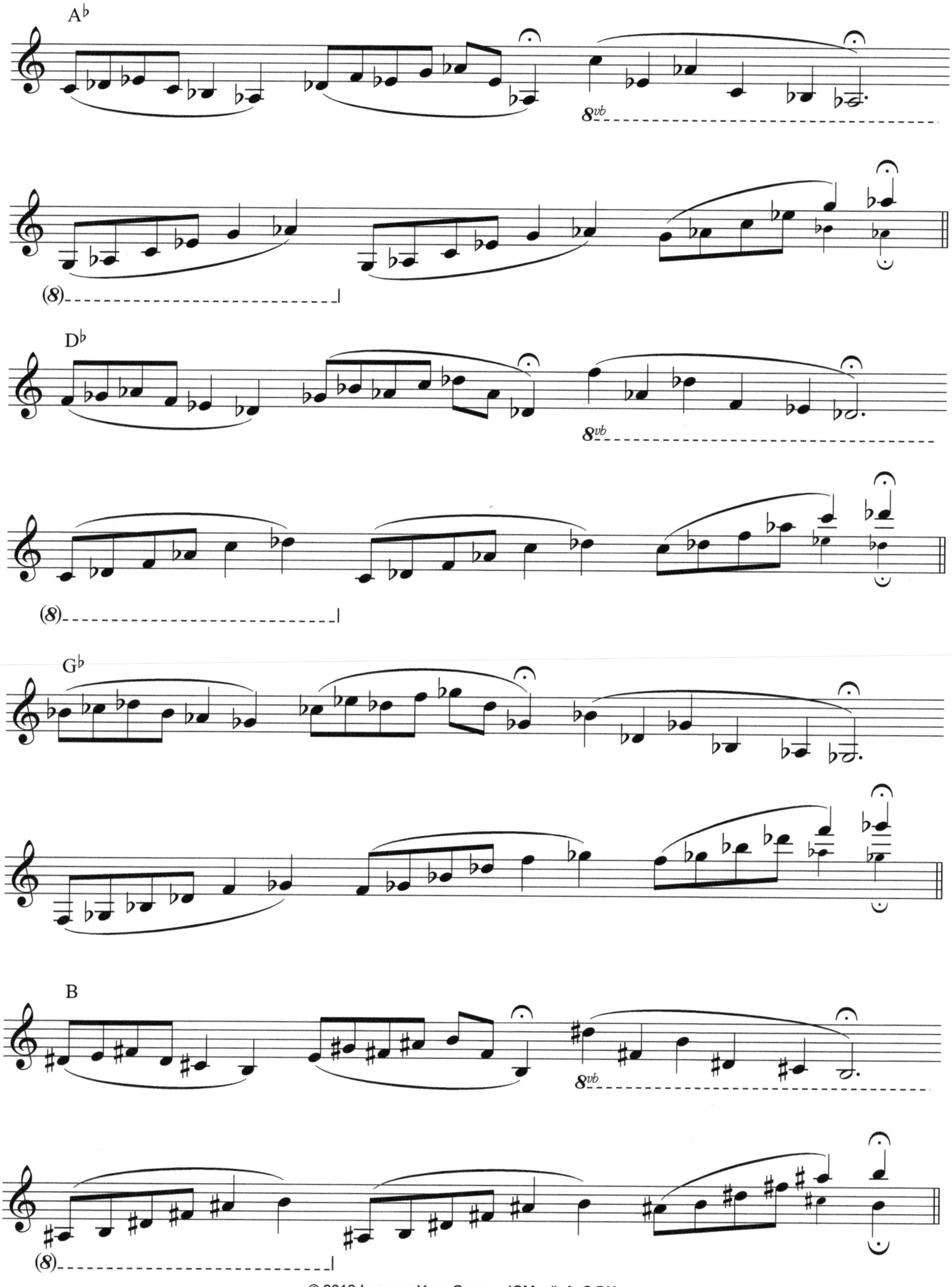
A♭
8vb
(8)
D♭
8vb
(8)
G♭
B
8vb
(8)

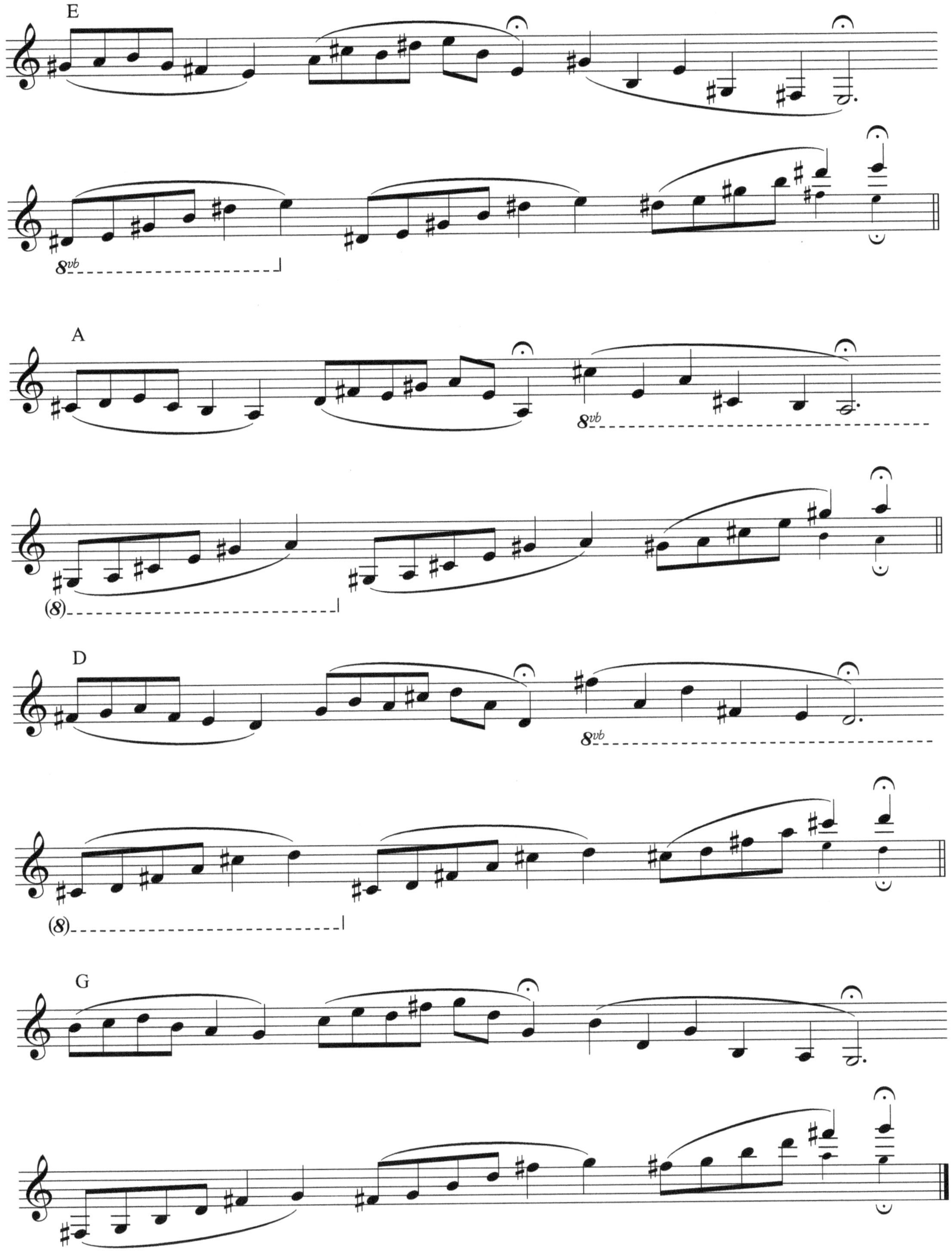
E
8vb
A
8vb
(8)
D
8vb
(8)
G

Daily Slurs - Week 04

Conclusion:

Cool down phrase

Take a 5-10 minute break and do something crazy

Now we're cranking it up a notch!

Daily Routine - Week 05

(Please read "Introduction to chapters" for reference - see index)

42

© 2012 Improve Your Game - JGMusik ApS DK

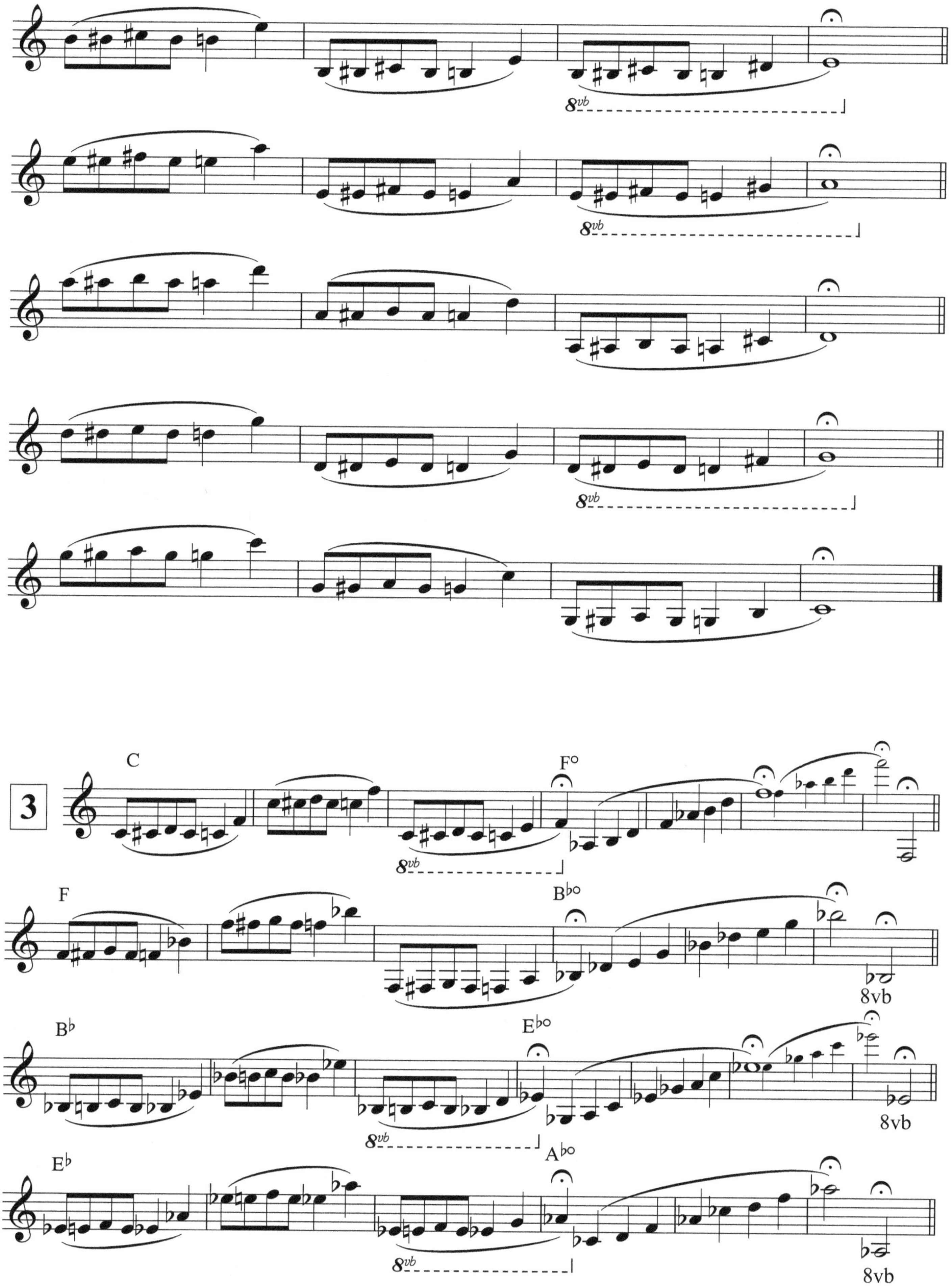
8vb
8vb
8vb
3
C
F°
8vb
F
B♭°
8vb
B♭
E♭°
8vb
8vb
E♭
A♭°
8vb
8vb

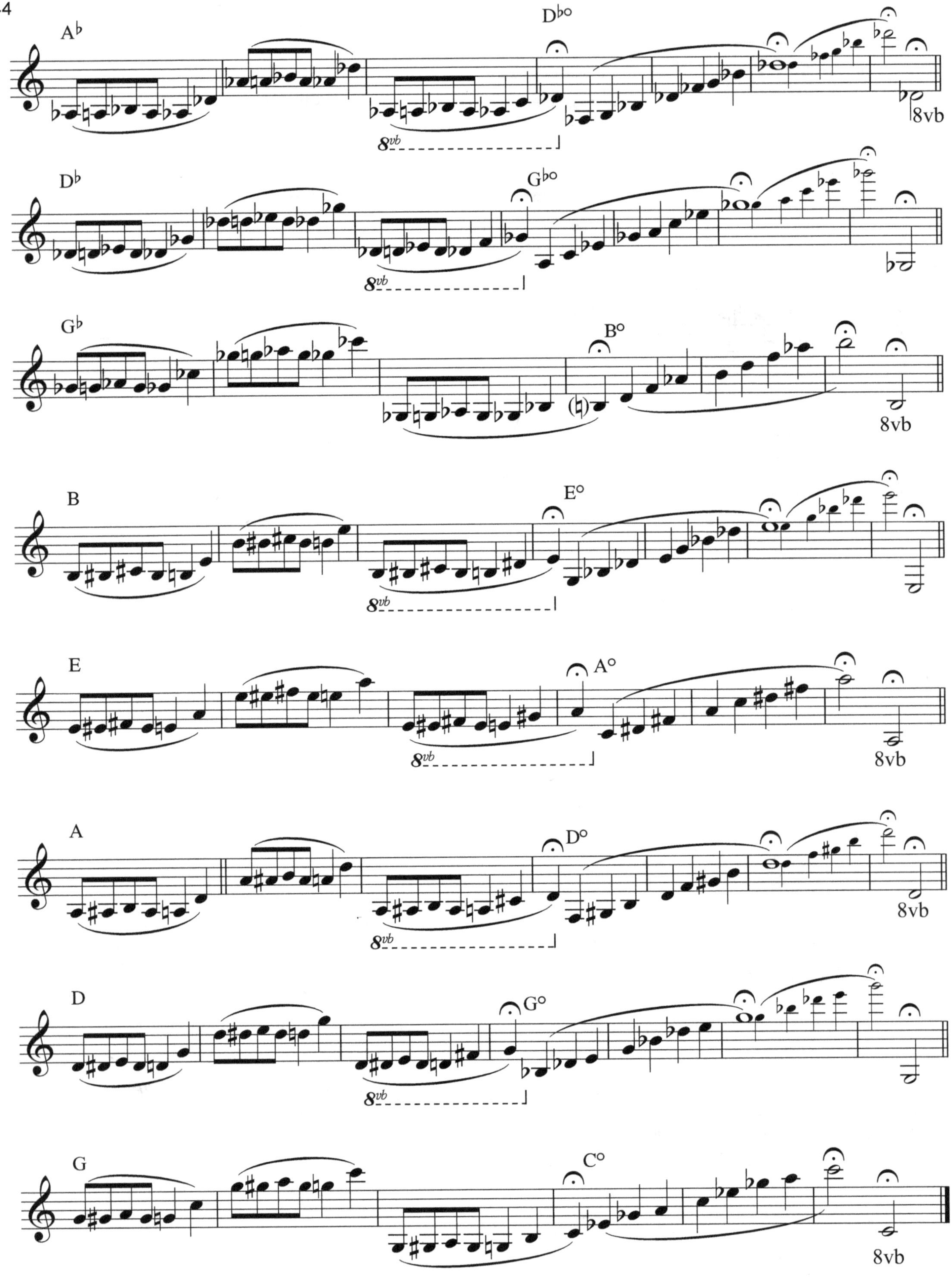

Take a 5-10 min break before continuing. Have a cup of coffee.

Daily Slurs - Week 05

Conclusion:

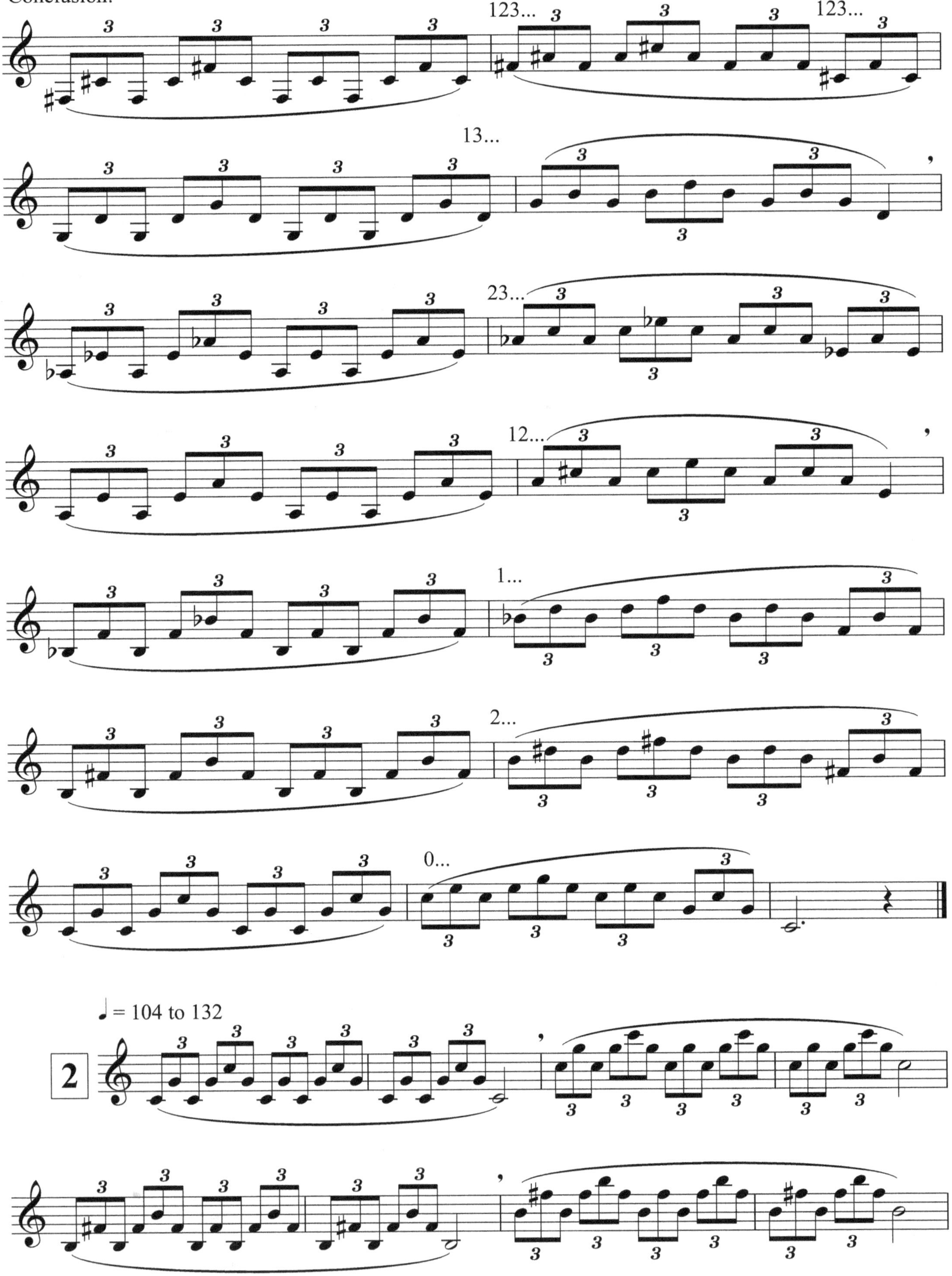

Conclusion:

Cool down phrase

Take a 5-10 minute break before continuing. Hug the wife or pet the dog. Or both! :)

Daily Routine - Week 06 - Endurance Part I

(Please read "Introduction to chapters" for reference - see index)

Rest as needed between each key.

♩ = 90

From here on, there are no more pedal-tones. That's why every key ends with tonic - 5th - tonic.

Take a 10-15 minute break and something that has nothing to do with playing the trumpet

Daily Routine - Week 06 - Endurance - Part II

Rest as needed between each key.

52

You can continue higher if you want. I'm happy with my high G.   :-)

Finally - soften your lips with this exercise

Rest for at least 20 minutes before contnuing. Have a cup of coffee. Good job!!!

Still not cracking walnuts with your lips? Don't worry - you will!!!

53

Daily Routine - Week 07

(Please read "Introduction to chapters" for reference - see index)

54

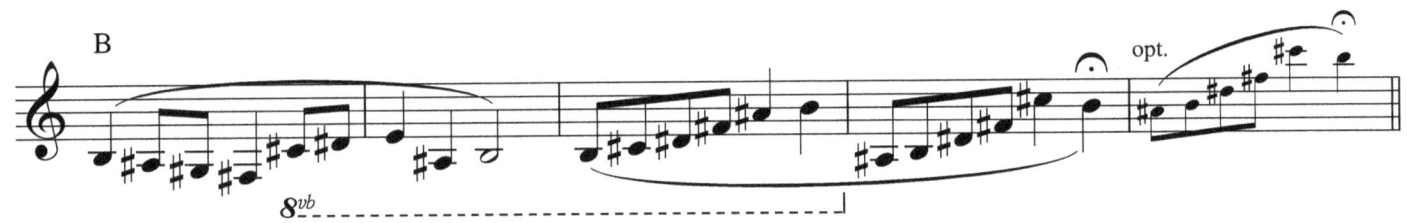

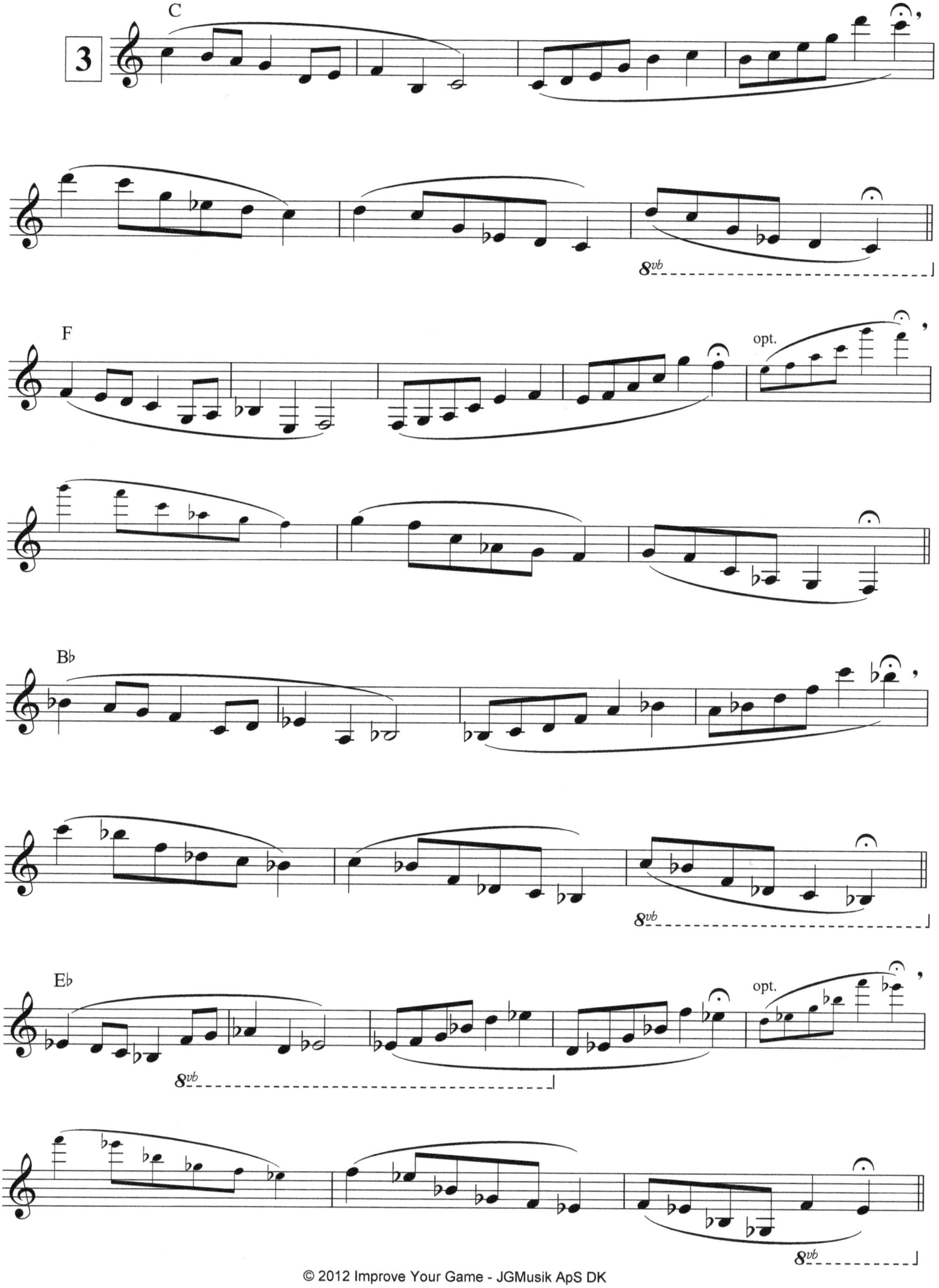
3
C
8vb
F
opt.
B♭
8vb
E♭
8vb
opt.
8vb

56

© 2012 Improve Your Game - JGMusik ApS DK

Rest 10 to 15 minutes before continuing.

Daily Slurs - Week 07

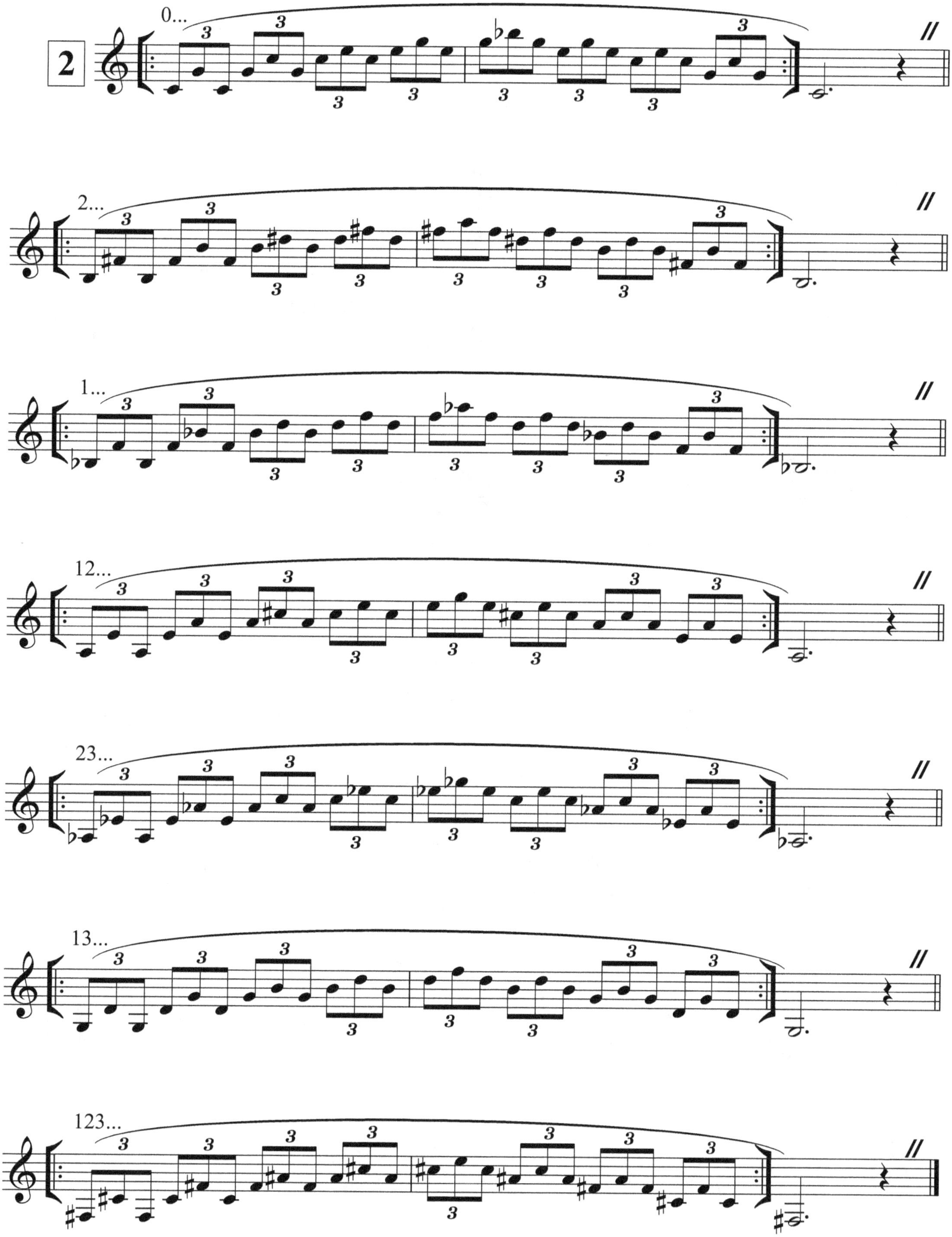
2
0...
2...
1...
12...
23...
13...
123...

60

Conclusion

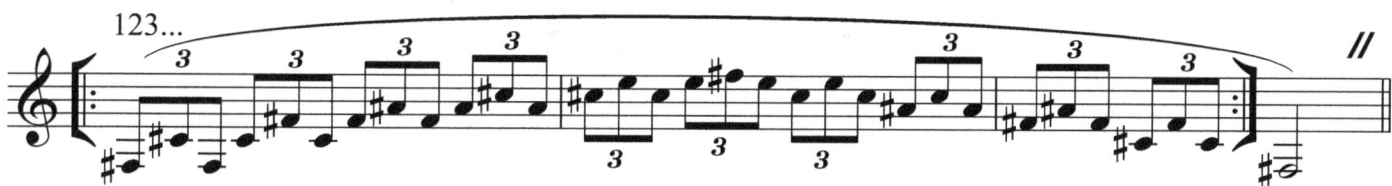

Conclusion

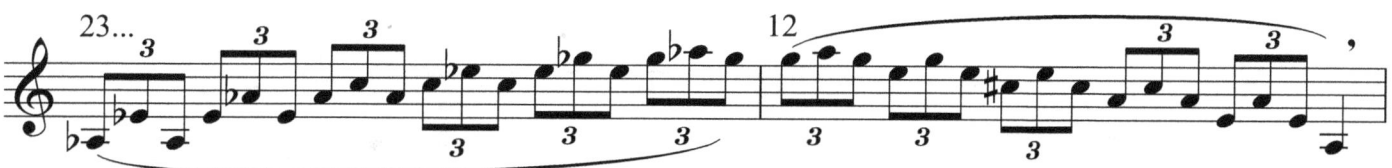

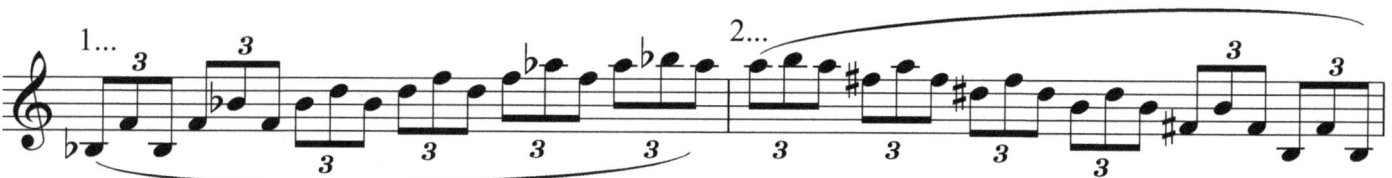

Take a short break before continuing.

This is Macho!!

Daily Routine - Week 07 -Expanding Major Scales

(Please read "Introduction to chapters" for reference - see index)

63

Simile...........................

Simile.......................

Simile.......................

Simile.......................

Cool down phrase

Rest 5-10 minutes before continuing.

Now you're gettin' the hang of it!!

Daily Routine - Week 08

(Please read "Introduction to chapters" for reference - see index)

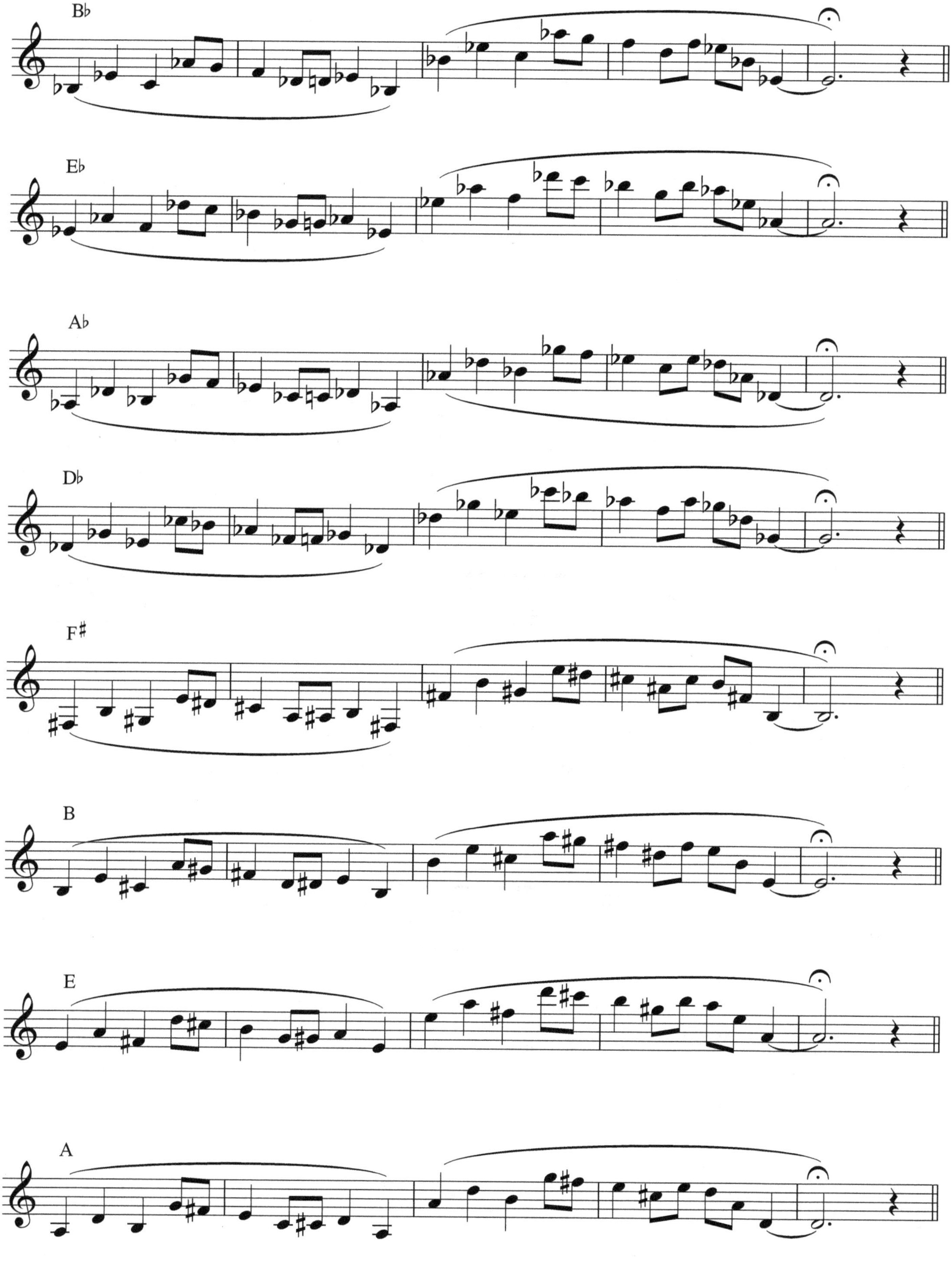
B♭
E♭
A♭
D♭
F♯
B
E
A

66

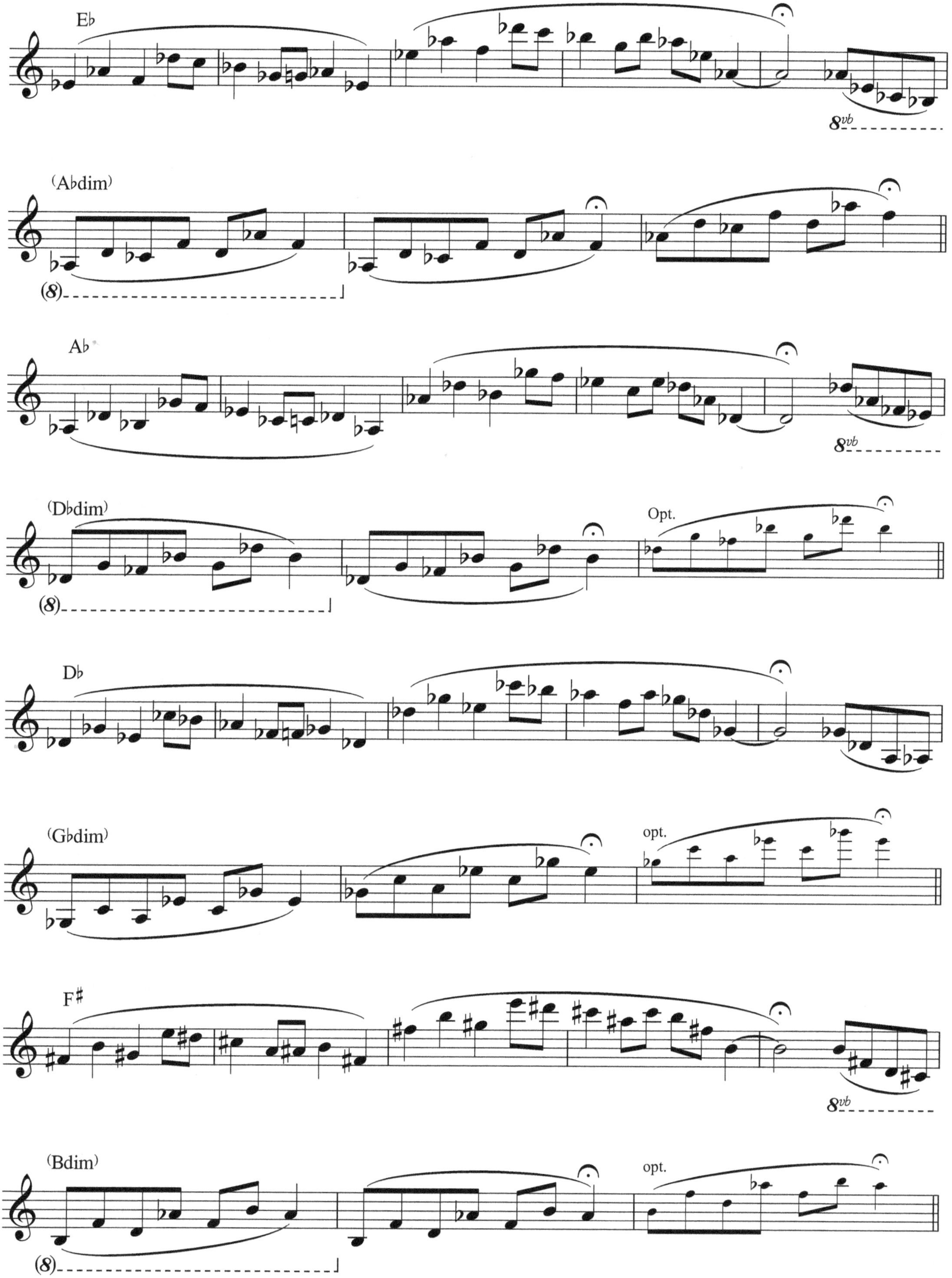
E♭
8vb
(A♭dim)
(8)
A♭
8vb
(D♭dim)
(8)
Opt.
D♭
(G♭dim)
opt.
F♯
8vb
(Bdim)
(8)
opt.

68

Rest 10 to 15 minutes before continuing.

Daily Slurs - Week 08

♩ = 132 or faster

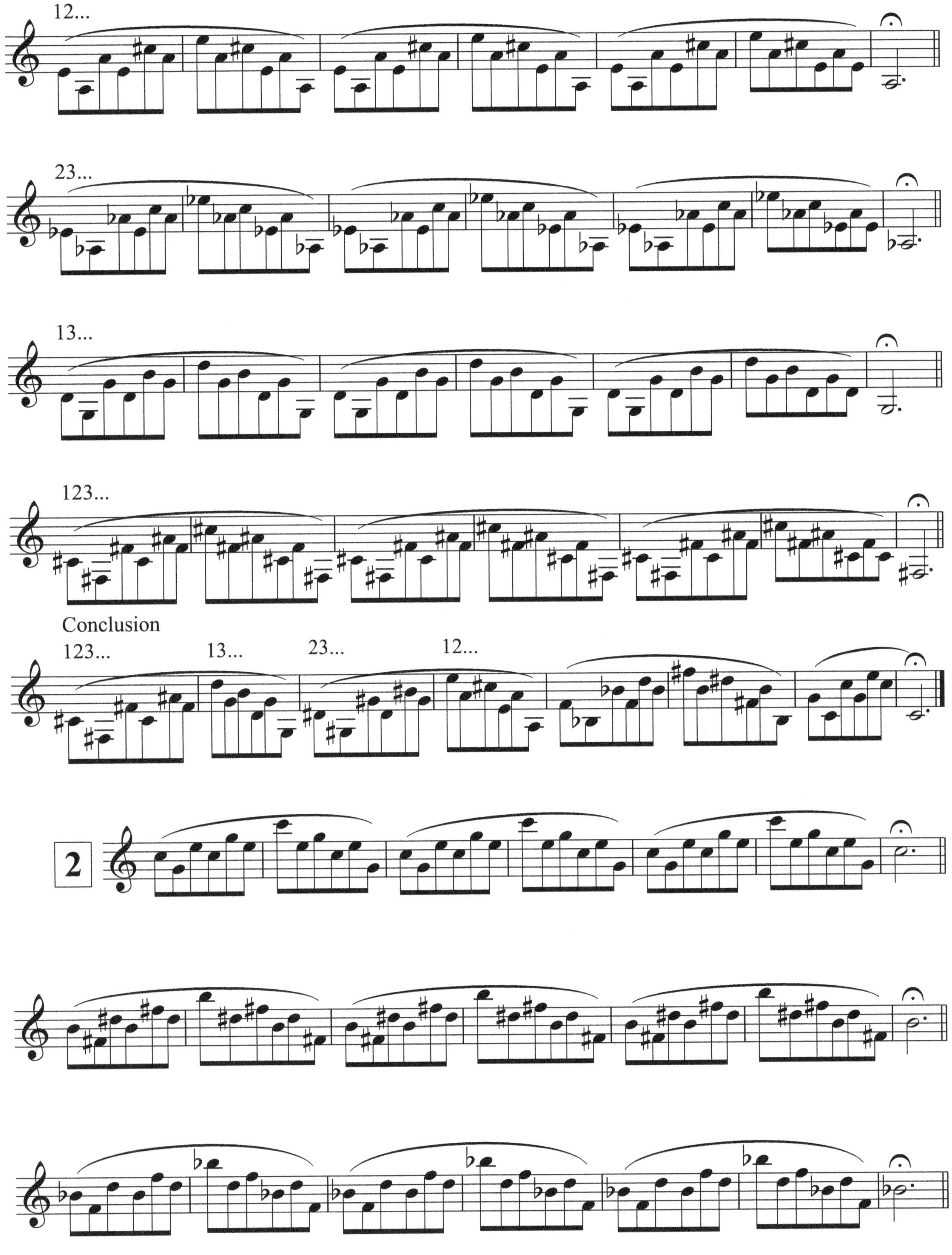
12...
23...
13...
123...
Conclusion
123...
13...
23...
12...
2

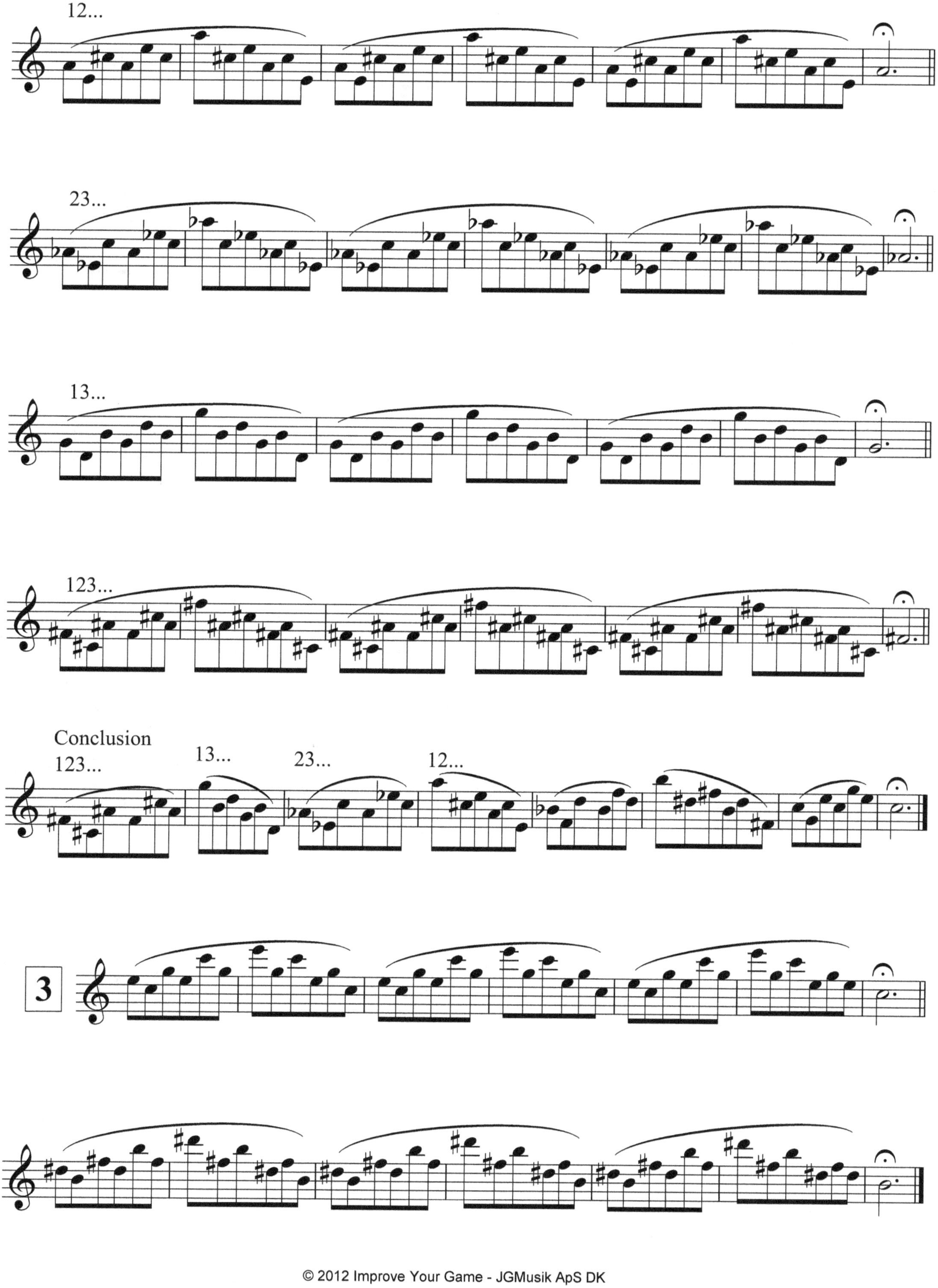
12...
23...
13...
123...
Conclusion
123...
13...
23...
12...
3

Rest 10-15minutes before continuing. You need it!!

Now it's really getin' tough

Daily Routine - Week 09

(Please read "Introduction to chapters" for reference - see index)

74

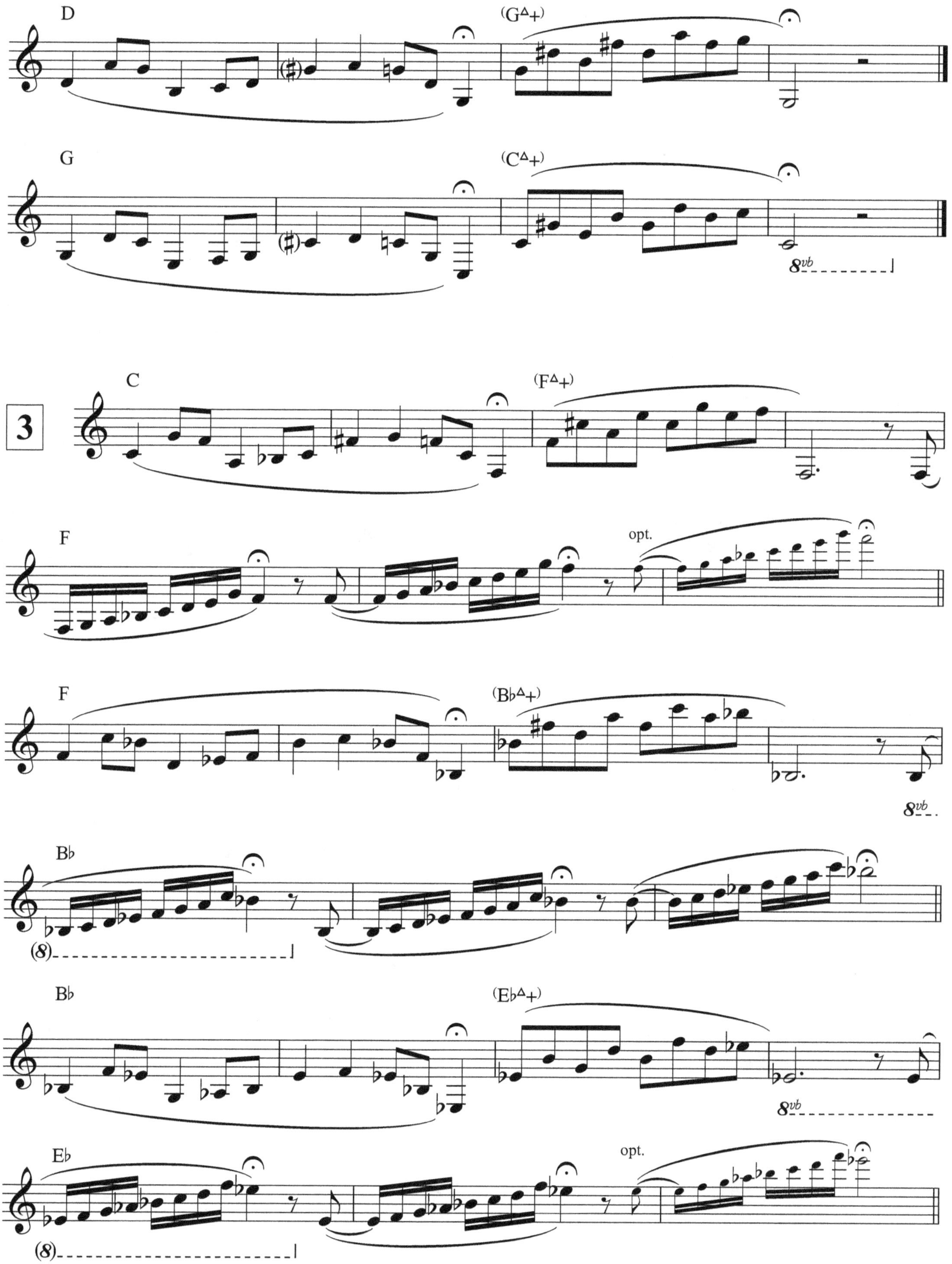
D
(GΔ+)
G
(CΔ+)
8vb
3
C
(FΔ+)
F
opt.
F
(B♭Δ+)
8vb
B♭
(8)
B♭
(E♭Δ+)
8vb
E♭
opt.
(8)

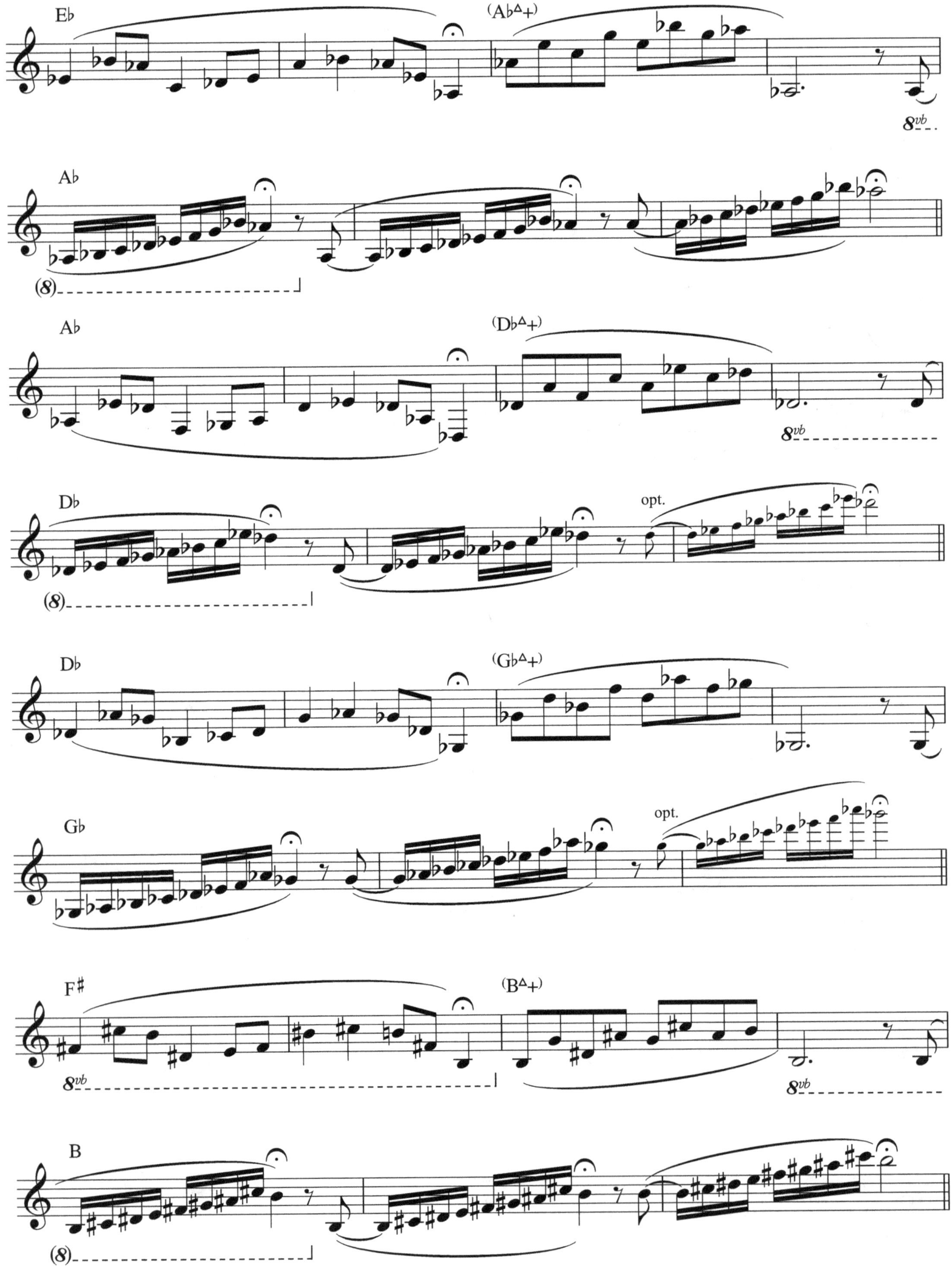
E♭
(A♭△+)
8vb
A♭
(8)
A♭
(D♭△+)
8vb
D♭
opt.
(8)
D♭
(G♭△+)
G♭
opt.
F♯
(B△+)
8vb
8vb
B
(8)

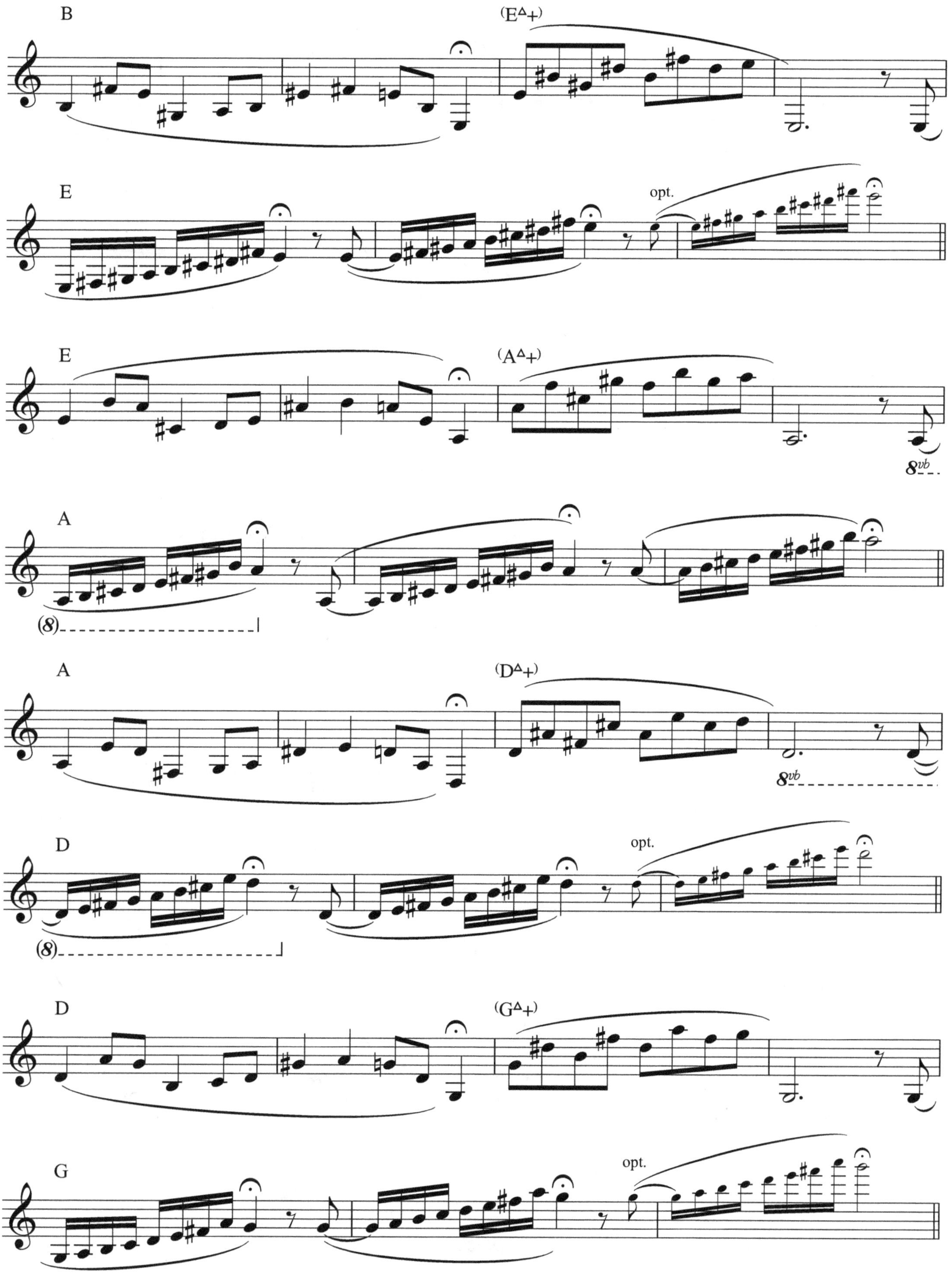
B
(EΔ+)
E
opt.
E
(AΔ+)
8vb
A
(8)
A
(DΔ+)
8vb
D
(8)
opt.
D
(GΔ+)
G
opt.

Rest 10 to 15 minutes before continuing. The end is near!!!

Daily Slurs 1 - Week 09

Expanding Chromatic Scales - Two Octaves

*extention 1

Simile like vers. 1   *extention 2

*extention 3

etc.....

Simile.......

Simile.......

Simile.......

Simile.......

Simile.......

* exception

Daily Slurs 2 - Week 09

Expanding Chromatic Scales - Three Octaves

*extention 1

Simile like vers. 1   *extention 2

80

*extention 3

Simile.......

etc.....

Simile.......

Simile.......

Simile.......

Simile.......

Simile.......

* exception

Simile.......

Cool down phrase

Take a 10 minute break. You deserve it!!

After this - you're done!!

Daily Routine - Week 10

(Please read "Introduction to chapters" for reference - see index)

82

A
Lip trill
12
D
Lip trill
1
8vb
G
Lip trill
0
3
C
Lip trill
0
8vb
F
Lip trill
1
B♭
Lip trill
1

84

© 2012 Improve Your Game - JGMusik ApS DK

B
Lip trill
2
8vb
E
Lip trill
0
8vb
8vb
A
Lip trill
12
8vb
D
Lip trill
0
8vb

86

Lip trill

Cool down phrase

Rest 10 to 15 minutes before continuing. Good job!!

When you're done with this - you're through!

Daily Slurs - Week 10
Octave intervals using leading notes - Level I

Octave intervals using leading notes - Level II

Octave intervals using leading notes - Level III

Simile.......

Simile.......

Simile.......

Simile.......

Cool down phrase

Rest 5-10 minutes before continuing. Maintain you profile on Facebook

Practise Slowly

INTEGRATE TECHNIQUE
IT MUST SERVE A MUSICAL END.
PRACTISE
IS NOT OUR SOLE PURPOSE.
MUSICAL
PERFORMANCE IS THE GOAL.

Practise what troubles you, not what you already can do.

If you practise nothing else that day, be sure to follow the routine with at least a lyrical study.

When practising - always perform.

You play the way you practise.

Strive for 20 out of 20 times accuracy when practising a passage.

Practise with a friend!!

Make a list of your weaknesses and get to work on them.

Every note you play must be musical!!

WISE TRUMPET TAPAS - "PLAYING"

Endurance difficulties are usually due to tension in the breath

Sing and finger the passage you just completed while you rest

Play into the center of notes, think down. The center of notes are lower than you think.

Always commence with a clean attack and centre.

Nothing is so high that it can't be played an octave or two lower.

When performing, "hear" the music. leave the technical concerns in the practice room.

Hear the pitch before playing any note.

Keep throat open. Keep tongue down.

Slur everything first, then add articulations.

Nothing is so fast that it can't be played slower.

Exaggerate dynamics.

Lyrical Etudes - Level II

Jan Glaesel

Allegro Vivace

Jan Glaesel

Andante cantabile

Jan Glaesel

Jan Glaesel

Waltz For Trumpet

Jan Glaesel

My First Etude For Trumpet - F major

Jan Glaesel

Maestoso con brio

MY BOOKSHELF OF CONSTANT INSPIRATION

When I started to practice for real in 2004 the only method-book I had was:
J.S. ARBAN - COMPLETE CONSERVATORY METHOD FOR TRUMPET

This was the book I was handed back in 1967 when I join the Tivoli Boys Guard here in Copenhagen. I think it is considered one of the "bibles" for many trumpet players. In 2004 when I began my new journey I started collecting all kinds of trumpet method books. Here is a list of the content of "My bookshelf of constant inspiration", in random order.

Author	Title	Publisher
J.B. Arban	Complete Conservatory Method for Trumpet	Carl Fischer
Herbert L. Clarke	Technical Studies for the Cornet	Carl Fischer
Arturo Sandoval	Playing techniques & Performance Studies Vol. 1-3	Hal Leonard
James Stamp	Warm-Ups & Studies	Editions BIM
Claude Gordon	Systematic Approach to Daily Practice	Carl Fischer
Allen Vizzutti	The Allen Vizzutti Trumpet Method Vol. 1-3	Alfred Publishing
Geoff Winstead	The Real Way to Play the Cat Anderson Method	GWM Publishing
Carmine Caruso	Musical Calisthenics for Brass	Hal Leonard
Max Schlossberg	Daily Drills & Technical Studies for Trumpet	M. Baron Company
Gabriel Parés Parés	Scales for Cornet or Trumpet	Rubank - Hal Leonard
J.L. Small	27 Melodious and Rhythmical Exercises	Carl Fischer
David Vining	Ear training for Trumpet	Carl Fischer
John McNeil	Jazz Trumpet Techniques	Studio P/R
Charles Colin	Advanced Lip Flexibilities Vol. 1-3	Charles Colin Music
Charles Colin	Complete Modern Method for Trumpet or Cornet	Charles Colin Music
Jon Gorrie	High notes, Low Notes and Everything in Between	www.jongorrie.com

I've worked with all of these books and found, through them, inspiration for my own approach to trumpet playing. I pay my deepest respects to all of the writers, and it's with the utmost humility I've used them as inspiration for my version of the ultimate Trumpet Method Book.

MUSICAL STUDIES & ETUDES:

Musical studies and etudes are just as important as technical studies. Below you will find some of my favorite collections from my bookshelf. I divide my time between Technical Studies, Musical Studies and Etudes 50/50 - I urge you to do the same.

Author	Title	Publisher
Sigmund Hering	Thirty Etudes for Trumpet or Cornet	Carl Fischer
Sigmund Hering	Thirty-two Etudes for Trumpet or Cornet	Carl Fischer
Sigmund Hering	Forty Progressive Etudes for Trumpet	Carl Fischer
Kopprasch	Sixty Selected Studies for Trumpet	Carl Fischer
H. Voxman	H. Selected Studies for Cornet or Trumpet	Rubank - Hal Leonard
H. Voxman	H. Selected Duets for Cornet or Trumpet Vol. 1-2	Rubank - Hal Leonard
H. Voxman	Concert&Contest Collection for Cornet or Trumpet	Rubank - Hal Leonard
Larry Clark	Progressive Duets for Trumpet in Bb Vol. 1-2	Carl Fischer
Walter Beeler	Solos for the Trumpet-Player	G. Schirmer - Hal Leonard

CREDITS:

Most of all I want, I want thank my loving wife Miriam and the rest of my family for enduring the "awful" sound of practising the trumpet - Thanks guys!!

A special thanks goes to my good friend, and fellow trumpet player **Gary Cordell,** Las Vegas Nevada, for proofreading this project. Also thank you for introducing me to Tony Scodwell.

Tony Scodwell - my good friend and fellow trumpet player, for letting me play one of his fantastic handmade trumpets. "Tony - you're a true artist and craftsman building your fantastic horns."

Bob Reeves - mouthpieces. Thank you for taking almost a day out of your busy schedule to guide me to the mouthpieces which are going to follow me, for the rest of my life.

Jon Gorrie - for opening my eyes to the Print On Demand concept. Also for helping me setting up the whole online marketing side of the project - Let's do something more together.

Krogstrup & Hede - web bureau. For always doing your best for my websites.

Bithiah & Patrick Poulsen - Layout. I love the cover and all your input - thank you.

The Danish Musical Directors Union - for financial support.

Please feel free to contact me with feedback or questions at info@trumpetgame.com